KINGDOM DISCIPLESHIP

PART 2

MAKING DISCIPLES

L. Douglas Dorman, Ph.D.

LEADER SPACE

ALIGNING HEARTS WITH GOD'S PERSPECTIVE

TABLE OF CONTENTS

    A GLOBAL FOCUS
    There are four groups of people in our lives.
      1.Family members
      2.Friends
      3.Co-workers
      4.Community

Dedicated to Joan Dorman

PART 2—UNDERSTANDING THE BOOK OF ROMANS

J ESUS INSTRUCTS HIS followers to be on mission with him in the world, "Go Make Disciples of all nations," **Matthew 28:19 ESV** and the original disciples began immediately aligning their hearts with Jesus' words. Paul, although not a part of the original crew, takes the message of Jesus as his personal mandate; he gives his life to further the message to the ends of the earth. He pens a message for the church in Rome challenging them to push the message out. Paul's missional message for the first century church remain as pertinent in the 21st century as the latest podcast.

The book of Romans provides a missional map, a practical guide, moving followers of Jesus from being disciples to making disciples. In the first half of Romans, Paul tells us Jesus Christ rescues and restores those who **come** to him. In the second half of Romans, Paul outlines our call to **go** out in Jesus' name to rescue and restore others.

> "How then will they call on Him in whom they have not believed? How will they believe in Him whom they have not heard? And how will they hear without a preacher? How will they preach unless they are sent? Just as it is written, "HOW BEAUTIFUL ARE THE FEET OF THOSE WHO BRING GOOD NEWS OF GOOD THINGS!" **Romans 10:14-15 NASB**

My friend, Linus Morris, says, "Romans is meant to be interpreted literally, historically, and grammatically, but also relationally, redemptively, and missionally."[1] In 1988, Joan and I

---

[1] Dr. Linus Morris, *On Expedition Training*. Linus believes the path Paul puts forward in Romans unfolds spiritual development as being sequential, incremental, and iterative.

heard Linus teach through the book of Romans in Thousand Oaks, California. As he taught, I began to understand God's grace at a deeper level. Many churches and seminaries teach interpreting the Bible literally, historically, and grammatically, but fail to realize or actualize the second half, "relationally, redemptively, and missionally". The second part of Linus' list highlights the outworking of God's grace in and through his church.

Paul sees the journey with Jesus as a grace oriented community activity; grace finds its home in relationships. Jesus activity of redeeming humanity plays out both as an event and a process. Paul writes not only as a theologian but also as a Cross-cultural worker. Romans is Paul's opus; it is his heart message.

Like the yellow brick road in *The Wizard of Oz* the pages of Romans unfold for us a missional map. Paul tells us how to live the life of faith—the life we've always wanted. He outlines a path to get us unstuck and keep us moving forward to fulfill his purpose of filling the earth with the knowledge of the glory of the LORD.

Walking with Jesus is not a solo sport. In Romans 12, Paul emphasizes the importance of understanding our wiring and being a part of a missional team. Paul closes his letter with a list of leaders' names—women comprise 25 percent of the names on his list. God wants to empower and release women and men, old and young, children and teens, to flood the earth with the fame of his name.

Ask the Holy Spirit to speak to you as you work your way through the book of Romans. Ask him to open your eyes and give you ears to hear so you can join God in his global adventure.

WEEK 1—DAY 1 INTRODUCTION—THE INDIFFERENT

THE KEY WORD: "INDIFFERENT".

THE KEY POINT: "SOCIETY SPIRALS DOWNWARD WITHOUT JESUS CHRIST."

ROMANS

- Paul penned Romans around 57 AD.
- Romans unfolds sequentially, and purposefully.
- Paul wrote 13 of the 27 New Testament books.
- Paul sent letters to four individuals & to nine regional or city churches.
- Paul hadn't visited the church in Colossae or Rome before writing them.[2]
- Romans contains Paul's heart message.
- Romans 1-8 invites us to "Come" to him; & Romans 9-16 tells us to "Go" global.
- Romans leads you to take Your Next Step in God's missional adventure.

ROMANS MAP

Study the Roman's Map below. Read each quadrant starting with **Bring** and work your way around clockwise. After you feel you've grasped the flow, reproduce the Romans Map in your journal.

---

[2] The books of Colossians and Romans.

The top half of the circle focuses on **Come** and the bottom half on **Go**. When we come to God, we become his disciples. As we mature in our faith, God sends us to go and make disciples. Like the ebb and flow of the ocean, our walk with God consists of coming to him, and going out to tell others about him. We repeat the symbols, colors, and concepts introduced in Part 1: Being a Disciple, here. Notice how Bring, Build, Send, Publicly and House to House evenly distribute into four chapters each: Bring—Romans 1-4, Build—Romans 5-8, Send—Romans 9-12, Publicly and House to House Romans 13-16.[3]

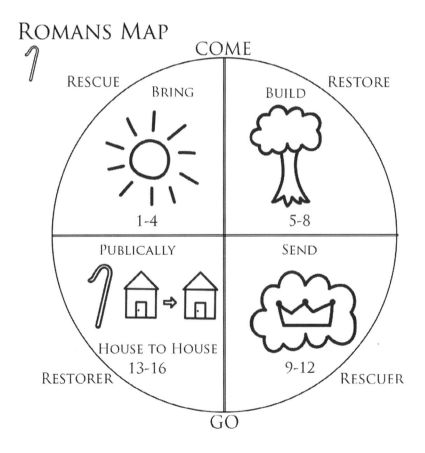

---

[3] See Appendix A for information about The Color Code and Symbols.

4

Take a few minutes and read Romans chapter 1 and journal your observations.

What patterns do you see?

What words are repeated?

Who is Paul addressing?

What argument does Paul present?

Go back now and read Romans 1:1-17 again. Jot down any additional observations.

The key verse is Romans 1:16 (ESV)

"For I am not ashamed of the gospel, for it is the power of God for salvation to everyone who believes, to the Jew first and also to the Greek."

Memorize Romans 1:16; the entire book of Romans hinges on this verse. Paul gives us his thesis statement in Romans 1:16. Write the verse in your journal.

Quote it when you meet with your one-on-one or small group this week.

Go back a few verses from Romans 1:16 to verses 5 and 8—Here Paul gives us the scope of his vision—**"all nations"**, **"the whole world."**

Have you traveled outside of your passport country? If so, where?

What part of the world do you feel drawn to?

Paul opens chapter 1 saying, "I am not ashamed"; he wants the whole world to know the good news of God's kingdom. Romans reveals God's heart to free the world from shame by the power of God. The world appears to be spinning out of control; however, God remains secure. God did not create the chaos around us; he created the world good, and humanity very good.

Humanity's rebellion against God set into motion pain, suffering, death, disease, and faulty world systems filled with corruption. God's plan includes setting the world to rights. Jesus came to declare a new kingdom and to rescue and restore those who come to him.

God desires to reverse the downward spiral of shame, fear, and guilt in our lives. To begin experiencing the divine reversal, we must recognize and honor God, by asking his forgiveness for our sin and receiving the gift of his son Jesus Christ. When we honor God, he removes our shame and restores our honor. God desires to rescue and restore us—SO WE CAN RESCUE AND RESTORE OTHERS.

Now, re-read Romans 1:18-31 again, to see why the world needs rescuing. Jot down your thoughts.

Romans 1:20 (ESV)
"For his invisible attributes, namely, his eternal power and divine nature, have been clearly perceived, ever since the creation of the world, in the things that have been made. So they are without excuse."[4]

Paul begins his argument by pointing out God's desire to reveal himself through nature. If you found a pristine Rolex watch while strolling on the beach, you'd not likely say, "Wow, look what time and chance produced." You'd assume, correctly, the watch had a designer. The sun, moon, and stars provide the world with a hint, "Someone created all this." Through creation God whispers to all of humanity, "Your life consists of more than time and chance. Seek the creator; the one who created you."

---

[4] Paul uses the concept of power distance, "His eternal power." In shame and honor cultures, the dominant worldview of Paul's audience, Paul points out God's power and humanity's powerlessness and dependence. The created world faces many limitations, including time and space. God knows no bounds; the creator's greatness far exceeds the world's finiteness. God is eternal; therefore, he deserves our gratitude and expressions of honor.

Societal Slide Downward

The pattern of the downward slide in Romans 1 moves from Indifference, to Idolatry or Idea-olatry, then Immorality, followed by Identity Confusion, and ultimately toward Insanity.[5]

Indifference

Romans 1:21 (ESV)

"For although they knew God, they did not honor him as God or give thanks to him, but they became futile in their thinking, and their foolish hearts were darkened."

THE INDIFFERENT—ROMANS 1

Romans 1 outlines society's movement away from God. Paul describes people's failure to honor God as God "or give thanks to him"; this failure begins a downward spiral. I remember my spiral away from God; I sat in Sunday School and stared out the window. A young boy, about my age, rode his skateboard up and down the hill at the apartments behind the church building. As I watched him zoom down the incline and push his board back up, I thought, "I'd rather be there than here."

I wasn't anti-God; I just felt indifferent toward him. God seemed irrelevant to me. My indifference led me in a direction away from God. I thought following God sounded boring.

Can you think of a time when you thought or acted indifferent toward God? Take a couple of minutes to journal about it.

Plan to share your story with someone this week.

---

[5] Dr. Linus Morris Sr. and Linus Morris Jr. in their book on Romans, *The Divine Expedition*, talk of the societal slide away from God. Those who fail to give honor to God begin a slide from Indifference, to Idolatry or Idea-olatry, Immorality, Identity Confusion, and ultimately, Insanity.

Idolatry or Idea-olatry

Romans 1:22 (ESV)

"And exchanged the glory of the immortal God for images resembling mortal man and birds and animals and creeping things."

God made humanity to enjoy his glory. However, all of humanity exchanged this glory for lesser things. For me, I did not set up a shrine with images in my room to burn incense before. No, I chose a poster of Farah Fawcett, and magazine shots of all my favorite surfers riding huge waves in Hawaii. Sports, mainly surfing, became the idea, "idea-olatry", I elevated above God.

Immorality

Romans 1:24 (ESV)

"Therefore God gave them up in the lusts of their hearts to impurity, to the dishonoring of their bodies among themselves."

In **Kingdom Discipleship—Part 1: Being a Disciple**, we talk about **Walking in Freedom**. I share about my lustful patterns. The picture of Farrah indicates the unhealthy pattern of viewing women as objects. At times the spiral works more like a pinball machine, bouncing between indifference, idea-olatry, and immorality. Each time we choose to yield to an object rather than the creator our bondage increases, like the score on the pinball game.

God Gave Them Up

Paul uses the phrase "God gave them up" three times in verses 26-28. When we turn away from God, he gives us up, or over to our choices; but he does not give up on us. In other words, God turns us over to the consequences of our own choices. The first two times Paul uses the phrase, "God gave them up", he links the concept directly to the loss of human honor or dignity. God gives us up to our own devices so he can show his mercy toward us when we turn to him. You have heard of hitting rock bottom; Paul develops this concept in Romans 1.

Identity Confusion

Romans 1:26-27 (ESV)
"For this reason God gave them up to dishonorable passions. For their women exchanged natural relations for those that are contrary to nature; and the men likewise gave up natural relations with women and were consumed with passion for one another, men committing shameless acts with men and receiving in themselves the due penalty for their error."

Around the same time I played spiritual pinball, an older teenage boy in our neighborhood exposed himself to me. I remember feeling really confused. I thought, "Wait, I'm attracted to girls," but, "Maybe I'm gay." My sexual confusion did not last long, but it fueled my appetite to prove my maleness by increasing my lustful objectification of women.

Insanity

Romans 1:28 (ESV)
"And since they did not see fit to acknowledge God, God gave them up to a debased mind to do what ought not to be done."

The third use of "God gave them up" also ties in with shame, the lack of honor, using the word "debased."

Romans 1:29 -31 (ESV)
"They were filled with all manner of unrighteousness, evil, covetousness, malice. They are full of envy, murder, strife, deceit, maliciousness. They are gossips, slanderers, haters of God, insolent, haughty, boastful, inventors of evil, disobedient to parents, foolish, faithless, heartless, ruthless."

Although I did not go insane, I did move down the list and started stealing, lying, cursing, and cheating my way through school.

I began banking all the money I could and would troll through Myrtle Beach checking vending machines, game machines, telephone booths and searching the cushions of furniture (My parent's owning motels helped me acquire some wealth).[6] I worked as many jobs as I could to save more money. The love of money gripped me. By the time I was 14, my dad came to me and asked if he could borrow money from me to pay his taxes, true story. My life focused on girls, gold, and glory. However, my self-centered life could not fill the hole of loneliness I felt in my soul.

God's Wrath

Romans 1 paints a picture of the downward slide of those indifferent toward God. God's present wrath, the here and now variety, refers to the natural consequences of a life lived independent of God. When we reject God's rule and reign in our lives, life does not work; we experience God's displeasure. God desires to use the dissatisfaction to woo us toward him, but most of us run in the other direction.

Those who refuse to repent by turning away from lesser things toward God, will face not only the current wrath of God, the consequences of their own making, but also will face future wrath— eternal separation from God. God allows his creation to reject him. God does not force himself on us. If we do not want God's rule and reign in our lives, God will allow us to live eternally apart from him.

If the story ended in Romans 1, the story would truly be bleak, a terrible tragedy. However, the play is just beginning. The good news of the kingdom unfurls the heart of God to reverse the downward spiral of sin and shame. The movement from indifference, to idolatry or idea-olatry, immorality, identity confusion, and insanity, is reversible. The reversal begins when we honor God and give thanks.

Review the list . . .
- Indifference
- Idolatry or Idea-olotry
- Immorality
- Identity Confusion
- Insanity

---

[6] Telephone booths were an ancient method of communication used by earthlings.

JOURNAL TIME

In what ways have you been indifferent toward God?

How did indifference lead to other steps away from God?

How do you see a downward spiral in society?

When you think of the downward spiral in society, how would you visually depict it?

Draw the downward spiral you see around you in your journal and share it with someone this week.

Week 1—Day 2
The Moral—Romans 2

The Key Word: "Moral".

The Key Point: "The Moral sit in judgment of the indifferent."

Read Romans 2:1-11 and write down in your journal at least three observations.

In Romans 1 we clearly observe the downward spiral from indifference to insanity. Paul describes society's self-seeking bent. When we get to chapter two, we move from the indifferent self-seekers to the moral self-seekers. The moral person looks down on the people in chapter 1; the moralist stands in judgment of the indifferent and immoral folks. Good people, moral people condemn the behavior of the immoral people they know. Moral people express relief since they don't behave like the people described in chapter 1. Moralists rely on their goodness; their self-righteous pride comes with a subtle hint of superiority.

Romans 2:1 (ESV)
"Therefore you have no excuse, O man, every one of you who judges. For in passing judgment on another you condemn yourself, because you, the judge, practice the very same things."

13

Have you ever driven down the road and yelled at someone who pulls out in front of you? "Idiot, where did you learn to drive?" Then, three blocks later, you need to get over in the right hand lane and you quickly slide over, no signal, no warning, and the car behind you blows the horn. I bet I know what the second car is yelling. Paul says those who judge, "Practice the very same things."

The moral seeks to establish their own goodness but fails—they "have no excuse."

Moral people may say, "I'm not perfect, but I'm not as bad as Tom." Or, I may tell a white lie occasionally, but I've never robbed a bank." The moral pass judgment on others. They never compare themselves to those better than them. After all, they are no saint. The moralist misunderstands God's kindness, not knowing his kindness, not their goodness, makes one righteous. Righteousness comes by faith not by our goodness.

Romans 2:4 (ESV)
"Or do you presume on the riches of his kindness and forbearance and patience, not knowing that God's kindness is meant to lead you to repentance?"

The moralist exchanges relationship for rules and in so doing pushes others away from them and from God. The moral person reminds me of someone who steps in dog poop but thinks the smell comes from those around them.

To reflect the character of God, we must show kindness to those far from him.

Romans 2:5 (ESV)
"But because of your hard and impenitent heart you are storing up wrath for yourself on the day of wrath when God's righteous judgment will be revealed."

In Romans 1 we see present wrath as the consequence of not honoring God. Here in chapter 2, Paul speaks of future wrath, "storing up wrath."

When I was a kid, I often got in trouble at school. I would receive the present wrath of my teachers while at school. However, I knew there would be a future wrath as well. The school would call my parents to inform them I received disciplinary action at school. When I got home, I received additional discipline. At school, I was storing up wrath for later.

We can be spared God's wrath, but not if we justify ourselves. We must check our own shoes. God desires to restore glory and honor. As we honor God, he pours out honor on us as well.

Romans 2:6-11 (ESV)

"He will render to each one according to his works: to those who by patience in well-doing seek for glory and honor and immortality, he will give eternal life; but for those who are self-seeking and do not obey the truth, but obey unrighteousness, there will be wrath and fury. There will be tribulation and distress for every human being who does evil, the Jew first and also the Greek, but glory and honor and peace for everyone who does good, the Jew first and also the Greek. For God shows no partiality."

Romans 2:6-11 contains several shame and honor concepts. God gives retribution—those who do well receive glory and honor, and those who fail to obey God, the self-seeking, receive wrath. Our problem stems from not honoring God and seeking to justify ourselves, "I'm not as bad as _____."

Read Romans 2:12-29.

The second half of Romans 2, continuing through Romans 3, introduces religious people.[7] Paul exposes the hypocrisy of religious ritual devoid of true faith calling it "dishonorable." God wants our hearts not just ritualistic motions.

In *Kingdom Discipleship—Being a Disciple*, we introduced The Three Trees illustration—repeated here.

---

[7] James 1:27 speaks of pure and undefiled religion—visiting orphans and widows, and walking in purity. Religion as we use it here, refers to those who seek to establish righteousness with God through their observance of rituals.

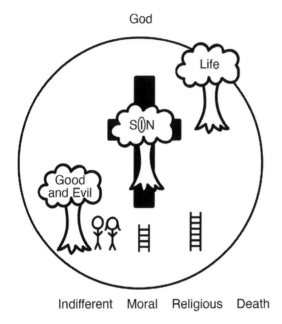

God

Life

S(I)N

Good and Evil

Indifferent   Moral   Religious   Death

In Romans 1, we see those indifferent to God. In Romans 2, we meet the moral and religious people.

The first ladder represents the moral person; they express gladness for being better than the indifferent. But notice the second ladder, the religious ladder reaches higher. The religious look down on both the moralist—they don't go far enough—and on the indifferent because they go too far in the wrong direction. However, neither the moralist nor the religious can reach the height of God's righteousness.

In Romans 5, Paul says,

Romans 5:8 (NASB)
"But God demonstrates His own love toward us, in that while we were still sinners, Christ died for us."

Jesus died for the indifferent, the moral, and the religious, all of those who seek to establish their own righteousness. Romans 4 reveals how God's righteousness becomes ours, the scandal of grace, but I'm getting ahead of myself. To summarize Romans chapter 2 . . .

The moral person holds themselves up as the standard, but they cannot keep their own standards.

The religious seek to regain honor by following written codes or oral traditions, but they fail, missing the heart of God by replacing relationship with God for rules about God.[8]

Romans 2:23 (ESV)
"You who boast in the law dishonor God by breaking the law."

God is after our hearts not merely obedience to our own standards or even legal statues.

Romans 5:29 (ESV)
"But a Jew is one inwardly, and circumcision is a matter of the heart, by the Spirit, not by the letter. His praise is not from man but from God."

In chapter 3, we continue to see the religious persons' attempts to justify themselves.

---

[8] **A life characterized by religious rules . . . Luke 18:9-17**
Fasted twice a week, tithed, accusation, judgment, anger, hard work, keep the commands, principals, no celebration.

A life characterized by repentant relationship . . . Luke 15 The prodigal son
Grief over loss, seeking, freedom even to choose wrongly, rejoicing, friends and neighbors, food, dancing, music, party time.

JOURNAL TIME

In what ways do you act as a moralist?

How do you sit in judgment of others?

Draw The Three Trees illustration.

When you look at your life, what do you see? Are you indifferent, moral, or religious? In what ways?

Write about your experience. How do you fail to keep your own standards?

How have rules replaced relationship in your life?

Week 1—Day 3
The Religious—Romans 3

The Key Word: "Religious"

The Key Point: "The religious judge the immoral and moral as inferior to them."

Read Romans 3:1-8

Paul continues to outline the religious life.

Romans 3:3 (ESV)

"What if some were unfaithful? Does their faithlessness nullify the faithfulness of God?"

The indifferent, the moral and the religious all fail to honor God. They demonstrate unfaithfulness, all of them and all of us. The honorable person realizes God alone demonstrates faithfulness.

Romans 3:7-8 (ESV)

"But if through my lie God's truth abounds to his glory, why am I still being condemned as a sinner? And why not do evil that good may come?—as some people slanderously charge us with saying. Their condemnation is just."

In contrast to our failure to show honor, here called "my lie," God's glory shines.

Some people reason, since they can't measure up, they will just give themselves over to their passions, comparisons, or judgments.

A friend of mine recently shared about his journey to Jesus. In high school he got a girl pregnant. She decided to abort the child. He responded by becoming even more rebellious thinking, "If I'm going to hell anyway, why not enjoy the trip." He bought into "the lie."

Read Romans 3:9-20

Romans 3:10 (ESV)
"As it is written; None is righteous, no, not one;"

No one is righteous.
Think of the best person you know—No, not even her or him.

Read Romans 3:21-31

Romans 3:21-23 (ESV)
"But now the righteousness of God has been manifested apart from the law, although the Law and the Prophets bear witness to it—the righteousness of God through faith in Jesus Christ for all who believe. For there is no distinction: for all have sinned and fall short of the glory of God."

All fall short—The indifferent, the moral and the religious.

Romans 3:25 (ESV)
"Whom God put forward as a propitiation by his blood, to be received by faith. This was to show God's righteousness, because in his divine forbearance he had passed over former sins."

God puts forward a solution, propitiation[9]. He provides a substitute for humanity's failures. Jesus took our place of punishment.

Romans 3:27 (ESV)
"Then what becomes of our boasting? It is excluded. By what kind of law? By a law of works? No, but by the law of faith."

God's substitutionary gift removes our ability to claim our own honor.
No one can boast, all fall short.

---

[9] A payment, a replacement.

21

My friend who ran from God because of the abortion mentioned above, eventually surrendered his life to Jesus. He realized his own indifference toward God, his attempts to live life by his own moral standards and social climbing, and his religious attempts of church attendance, fell short of God's kindness. God outran him and he yielded to the pursuit of the lover of his soul. Grace consumed his sin by crediting him righteous (Tomorrow, we'll unpack credited righteousness).

JOURNAL TIME

What stands out to you in Romans chapter 3? Write down your observations, questions, and reflections.

How are you religious?

WEEK 1—DAY 4
COUNTED—ROMANS 4

Read Romans 4:1-12

THE KEY WORD: "COUNTED", "RECKONED", "CREDITED" DEPENDING ON TRANSLATION.

THE KEY POINT: THERE IS A RIGHTEOUSNESS OUTSIDE OF OURSELVES WHICH IS FOUND IN JESUS.

Have you ever heard someone say, "You can count on it." Well, Paul says this about our hope found in Jesus Christ. In fact, he says it a bunch of times. Go back through Romans 4:1-12 and count the number of times counted, reckoned, or credited is used.

In the original Greek, the word λογίζομαι (**logizomai**) translates as "counted." The New American Standard and the New International Version translate logizomai as "Credited"; The English Standard Version uses "Counted", and The King James Version says "reckoned". **How many times can you find where "credited" or "counted", or their cognates, appear?**

Circle or underline the word in your Bible and write down the number you come up with.

_____

In Romans 1, the indifferent count themselves right, or righteous, by doing what is right in their own eyes. In Romans 2, the moralist counts themselves righteous because they are not as bad as others. In Romans 3, the religious count themselves righteous because they keep the rules. However Romans 3 closes with Paul saying, "all fall short of the glory of God." All, the indifferent, the moral, the religious, ALL fall short.

Paul show's us a fourth way. Because of Jesus' death, righteousness is counted or credited to us.

Since all of the approaches mentioned in Romans 1-3 fail to produce righteousness, how can we be made right with our creator? Is there any hope.Can honor be restored? Yes, God reveals a divine reversal of the downward spiral by revealing a righteousness from above, outside of human merit.

God reveals a righteousness from above, outside or our indifference, moral code, or religious practices—Jesus is our righteousness.

Illustration

Picture going to the bank to make a payment on a large sum of money you borrowed. The banker looks up your account and announces, "You do not owe anything." You respond, "There must be a mistake." They look again and say, "The note here says, your debt is 'paid in full.'" As you slowly get up and walk away, they call out, "Wait a minute." Your heart sinks as you think, "I knew it could not be true." The banker smiles and informs you, "Not only is your debt paid, you have $10,000,000 dollars credited to your account with compounded interest."[10]

When you said yes to Jesus righteousness got "credited", "counted" into your spiritual bank account. You now possess a limitless deposit of righteousness.

Unlike the pursuit of the indifferent, the moral and the religious person, the repentant person realizes, righteousness comes from outside of themselves. We cannot earn right standing with God. Righteousness is not like karma, or merit; it is a free gift.

Romans 4:2 (ESV)

"For if Abraham was justified by works, he has something to boast about, but not before God."

Abraham had no room for boasting. Abraham realized righteousness cannot be obtained through human effort. Those who

---

[10] Linus Morris and Phil Graf use the banking illustration in their Divine Expedition training.

boast declare their own honor—a shameful act. Have you met those who focus on their own academic, financial, or physical accomplishments? People who brag about their achievements repel those around them—oblivious of how their self-praise repulses others. The following statement exposes such practice.

Proverbs 27:2 NASB
"Let another praise you, and not your own mouth; A stranger, and not your own lips."

Paul points us to a better way; he points us to Jesus.

Romans 4:6-9 (ESV)
"Just as David also speaks of the blessing of the one to whom God counts righteousness apart from works: "Blessed are those whose lawless deeds are forgiven, and whose sins are covered; blessed is the man against whom the Lord will not count his sin." Is this blessing then only for the circumcised, or also for the uncircumcised? For we say that faith was counted to Abraham as righteousness."

God bestows righteousness as a covering, as one's nakedness would be covered, thus making provision for our shame.

How do we access God's righteousness? We begin by admitting our own self justification fails. We ask God to forgive us of our indifference toward him, our attempts to be good, moral, on our own, and our religious pursuits. We surrender our lives to his goodness confessing our desire to know the resurrected Jesus Christ. We accept Jesus' death, burial, and resurrection as sufficient to credit me righteous.

Read Romans 4:13-25 a jot down a few observations.

Romans 4:15 (ESV)
"For the law brings wrath, but where there is no law there is
no transgression."

Jesus took our sin and shame upon himself on the cross. He
provided a way, a bridge, back to the Father. Jesus absorbs the wrath
of God, meant for us, upon the cross. Followers of Jesus do not need
to fear the wrath of God, Jesus received it for us. For those who do
not know the Father, a future wrath is being stored up, but not for
the believer.

Wrath is the result of our inability to keep the law and is a means
of shaming. Shame awaits those who do not honor God, but Jesus
took the shame of his followers away.

Romans 4:20 (ESV)
"No unbelief made him waver concerning the promise of
God, but he grew strong in his faith as he gave glory to God."

Notice Abraham gave "glory to God." Abraham, unlike the
society around him, honored God. And God, honored Abraham. The
restoration of an honorable life comes, when we receive a
righteousness from above.

The walk of faith brings glory to God. Glory is a synonym for
honor. God honored us by counting us righteous.

JOURNAL TIME

Write down how your life has changed since you received God's righteousness.

WEEK 1—DAY 5—REVIEW

Read Romans 1-4

The diagram below represents the four worldviews we find in Romans 1-4. Go clockwise. Romans 1, the indifferent, represents those who simply want to be happy. Romans 2, the moralist, shows people who hope their good deeds outweigh their bad deeds. Romans 3, the religious, want to be sure they check all the right boxes. However, Romans 4 is different, these people realize they need rescuing by someone other than themselves.

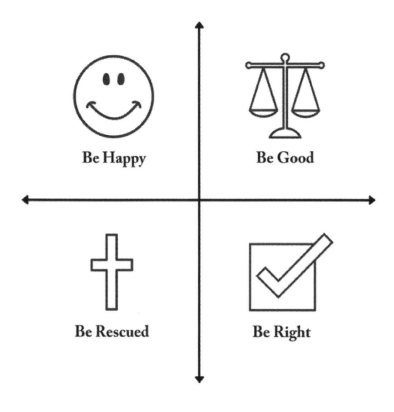

JOURNAL TIME

What stands out to you as you review this week's lessons?

Reproduce The Four Worldviews diagram.

Who can you share this with this week?

Week 2—Day 1
Treasures—Romans 5

The Key Word: "Treasures".

The Key Point: "His righteousness provides us with 10 treasures."

Read Romans 5

Romans 1-4 covers the 1st Quadrant of our Romans' map—Bring. In Romans 1, we see how the indifferent move away from honoring God. In chapter 2, we watch the moral stand in judgment of the indifferent. In chapter 3, we observe how the religious seek to keep the rules as a means of gaining merit. Then in chapter 4, we see Abraham step off of the crazy train, and put his trust in God's righteousness not his own.

We now move to the 2nd quadrant—Build. Once we receive God's righteousness, God begins to reverse the downward spiral of sin in our lives by building us up in him. After rescuing us and counting us righteous, he begins to restore us.

ROMANS MAP

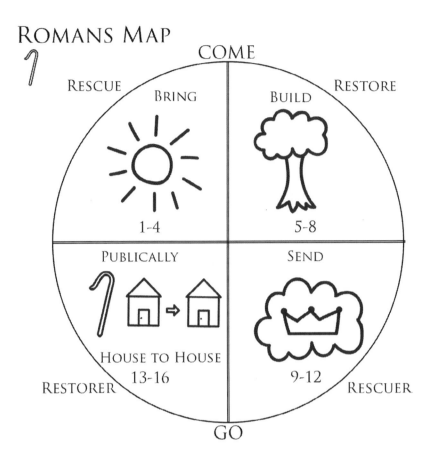

COME

RESCUE

RESTORE

BRING

BUILD

1-4

5-8

PUBLICALLY

SEND

HOUSE TO HOUSE
13-16

9-12

RESTORER

RESCUER

GO

Paul mentions "sin" 41 times in Romans 5-8. Genesis 4:7 records the first mention of the word "sin" in the Bible. God tells Cain "Sin is crouching at the door; and its desire is for you, but you must master it." However, Cain does not master sin; he yields to sin, and as a result sin masters Cain, and he takes his brother's life.

The enemy of our soul comes as a thief seeking to "steal, kill, and destroy" our lives as well; Jesus comes to give life, John 10:10. **Sin in Genesis 4 and in Romans 5-8 functions as an entity not an activity.**[11] Read the last sentence again. Think about it. Sin stands as an entity at your heart's door; it's desire is for you as it was

[11] See Hud McWilliams' book, *Discipline of Disturbance: Stop Waiting for Life to Be Easy*, 2018, Equip Press, Colorado Spring, Colorado page 149 for further explanation of sin as a noun.

for Cain. Those counted righteous can so no to the entity. When we allow the entity in the door, sinful behaviors follow. Check sin, the noun, at the door. Tell the thief he cannot enter, to be gone in Jesus' name.

In Romans 5-8, Paul outlines how God works to move his followers from rescue to restoration. God brings us into the kingdom and he then builds us up in him. Romans 1-4 tells of God's work of justifying us; Romans 5-8 outlines how he sanctifies us. The process of dealing with sin is less about sin management and more about spiritual warfare with our enemy "sin". Paul tells us in Romans 6 when we submit to sin, it becomes our master.

Romans 5:11 (NASB)
"And not only *this*, but we also celebrate in God through our Lord Jesus Christ, through whom we have now received the reconciliation."

When we receive God's gift of righteousness, God reconciles us to himself. He brings us out of the shame of isolation. Sin separates. But through Jesus, the Father welcomes us, we receive reconciliation with God.

The good news of the kingdom is reconciliation with God.

We receive a free-gift of salvation whereby we are justified before God.

Gift giving is foundational to the concept of honor. God provides the gift of his son, so we can be reconciled to the Father.[12]

The rescue and restoration process in Romans terraces like a waterfall from God's throne. God gives his Son to the world. We who receive him give honor to God. God honors us by giving us the gift of salvation. Jesus gifts us with his Holy Spirit and pours out special gifting on us. We use the God given gifts to honor God, and we begin honoring others as more important than ourselves. As we honor others, they give honor to God and the flow of his spirit spills out to the nations.

---

[12] See The Theological Dictionary of the New Testament, edited by Gerhart Kittel for an expansive understanding of honor. Honor and gift giving coincide in the Bible. God gives the gift of salvation through Jesus Christ. Jesus gifts his people to serve him effectively. When we honor God, he honors us with the gift of salvation and the gifts of the Holy Spirit.

Paul builds his entire case of justification by faith on the concept of God's provision for our sin through his honorable gift of Jesus Christ.

GOD HONORS YOU BY COUNTING YOU RIGHTEOUS.

Romans 5:1 (NASB)
"Therefore, having been justified by faith, we have peace with God through our Lord Jesus Christ."

THEREFORE . . . COUNTED

Notice the word "Therefore". When I was a teenager, I heard Bible teacher Derek Prince say, "When you see the word 'therefore' in the Bible, you should always ask, 'what is it there for?'" Paul uses "therefore" in Romans 5:1 to point us back to Romans 4:23-25—and to remind us God credits us . . . HE COUNTS US RIGHTEOUS! Therefore . . .

What is the "Therefore," there for? Well, because God credits us righteous, we have peace with God.

Draw a treasure chest in your journal.

Read Romans 5:1-5 and list the four treasures or benefits Paul gives as evidence of us being counted/credited righteous.

THE FOUR TREASURES

- Treasure # 1—Peace with God
- Treasure # 2—Grace in which we stand
- Treasure # 3—Hope of the glory of God
- Treasure # 4—Love poured out into our hearts

Peace, grace, hope and love are the first four treasures, or benefits, of walking by faith, but Paul tells us to expect "much more."
Therefore . . . JUSTIFIED
NOT BECAUSE OF OUR GOODNESS

Romans 5:9
Our Justification, right standing with God, provides much more than future salvation. We receive, already, salvation too, the kingdom rule and reign starts when we say yes to Jesus. Salvation comes already, and not yet; it is both an event, and a process. **Our salvation began in the past, continues in the present, and extends to the future. Read the last sentence again.**
You were saved from future wrath
You are being saved from sin's deception
You will be saved from the presence of sin, the entity—root and the activity—fruit.
God Created You for a life of "Much More"

Exercise
Read Romans 5:11-21. There are four more treasures which are identified as "much more." Jot down the references for the four "much mores" in your journal.

TREASURE # 5—MUCH MORE # 1— NO WRATH

God covers your sin removing your guilt, shame and fear. Since Jesus took the wrath of God on the cross, the follower of Jesus does not need to fear the future wrath of God.

Romans 5:9
"Since, therefore, we have now been justified by his blood, much more shall we be saved by him from the wrath of God."

TREASURE # 6—MUCH MORE # 2—HIS LIFE

God wires us for a love relationship with him. Out of the love relationship, we begin to live our lives for eternity and not time. Our concern shifts from self-focus to God-focus, how do we honor him?

Romans 5:10
"For if while we were enemies we were reconciled to God by the death of his Son, much more, now that we are reconciled, shall we be saved by his life."

TREASURE # 7—MUCH MORE # 3 ABUNDANT GRACE

God desires to show His love to others through you. Out of gratitude, not in order to gain approval but because we are approved, we seek to extend God's grace to those who do not yet know him.

Romans 5:15
"But the free gift is not like the trespass. For if many died through one man's trespass, much more have the grace of God and the free gift by the grace of that one man Jesus Christ abounded for many."

TREASURE # 8—MUCH MORE # 4—REIGN

God invites you to reign with him by seeing where he is at work and to join him. Listen more carefully when others speak. When those around us express need, or disclose personal information, they may be inviting us into their lives at a deeper level. Reigning with God prepares us to be agents of grace. Listen for God's whispers throughout the day. Obey his promptings and step into his invitations.

Has God invited you into a situation lately? Jot down your thoughts.

Romans 5:17

"For if, because of one man's trespass, death reigned through that one man, much more will those who receive the abundance of grace and the free gift of righteousness reign in life through the one man Jesus Christ."

JOURNAL TIME

Today, we introduced eight treasures. There are 10 total. Look back over the first eight treasures. Which treasure do you need most right now in your life? Write about it. Thank God for already providing the treasure. Ask him how you may access and appropriate his provision.

Share with your prayer partner or small group this week about the treasure you need most right now.

WEEK 2—DAY 2
A BATTLE TO FIGHT—
ROMANS 6

THE KEY WORD: "BATTLE"

THE KEY POINT: "THERE IS A BATTLE TO FIGHT."

Remember the second tree in The Three Trees illustration? Look back at the diagram on Week 1: Day 2 as a reminder. Notice, the second tree represents Jesus taking our sin upon himself.

Read Romans 6:1-14

Romans 6:1-4 (ESV)
"What shall we say then? Are we to continue in sin that grace may abound? By no means! How can we who died to sin still live in it? Do you not know that all of us who have been baptized into Christ Jesus were baptized into his death? We were buried therefore with him by baptism into death, in order that, just as Christ was raised from the dead by the glory of the Father, we too might walk in newness of life."

Baptism follows as one of the first acts of obedience for followers of Jesus. Paul points to the act of baptism to remind us, not only did Jesus die for us, but we died with him. "We were buried with him." Coming up out of the baptismal waters represents our new life. Picture baptism as a drama. The play opens with two people standing in the water. The individual receiving baptism is lowered into a watery grave, and rises with Christ into a new life.

Galatians 2:20 (NASB)
"I have been crucified with Christ; and it is no longer I who live, but Christ lives in me; and the *life* which I now live in the flesh I live by faith in the Son of God, who loved me and gave Himself up for me."

We died with Jesus, and we rose with him.

TREASURE # 9—NEW LIFE!

The ninth treasure reminds us our old life is buried, and we have a new life, a kingdom life. Our life no longer consists of the things we possess, the accomplishments we've achieved, or the failures we're ashamed of. We have a new life.

Romans 6:7, 9, 12-15-19, 21-23 (ESV)

7 "For one who has died has been set free from sin.

9 We know that Christ, being raised from the dead, will never die again; death no longer has dominion over him.

12 Let not sin therefore reign in your mortal body, to make you obey its passions.

13 Do not present your members to sin as instruments for unrighteousness, but present yourselves to God as those who have been brought from death to life, and your members to God as instruments for righteousness. 14 For sin will have no dominion over you, since you are not under law but under grace.

Read Romans 6:15-23

15 What then? Are we to sin because we are not under law but under grace? By no means! 16 Do you not know that if you present yourselves to anyone as obedient slaves, you are slaves of the one whom you obey, either of sin, which leads to death, or of obedience, which leads to righteousness? 17 But thanks be to God, that you who were once slaves of sin have become obedient from the heart to the standard of teaching to which you were committed, 18 and, having been set free from sin, have become slaves of righteousness. 19 I

am speaking in human terms, because of your natural limitations. For just as you once presented your members as slaves to impurity and to lawlessness leading to more lawlessness, so now present your members as slaves to righteousness leading to sanctification.

21 But what fruit were you getting at that time from the things of which you are now ashamed?

22 But now that you have been set free from sin and have become slaves of God, the fruit you get leads to sanctification and its end, eternal life. 23 For the wages of sin is death, but the free gift of God is eternal life in Christ Jesus our Lord."

The old life made us ashamed. Musician, Bob Dylan, said, "You gotta serve somebody." If we serve sin, it brings shame. If we serve God, it brings honor. The new life in Christ has set us free from a life of shame. God's grace is God's unmerited, unearned, favor.

Romans 6

Grace is not just unmerited favor . . .
Grace is the desire and power to do God's will
GRACE is: God's Riches at Christ's Expense
Should we continue in our old life once we've received a new life?
BY NO MEANS! Remember . . .

- You died to sin
- You were baptized into his death, buried
- You were raised- you have a new life
- Take Your Next Step Romans 6:4—New Life!
- You were united with Him
- Consider yourself dead to sin

Therefore: YOU HAVE A BATTLE TO FIGHT
Do NOT let sin reign in your life.

Romans 6:12

Go back to the old life . . . no way,
BY NO MEANS
How Can You Live It Out?

Present your body to God. Write out a prayer offering yourself to God.

Offer yourself as a servant to God, you are no longer to serve yourself. How do you envision serving God?

FREE GIFT . . . NO SHAME

We see 9 treasures God gave us through justification.[13]

- Peace
- Grace
- Hope
- Love
- MUCH MORE—No Wrath
- MUCH MORE—His Life
- MUCH MORE—Abundance
- MUCH MORE—Reign
- New Life

---

[13] Dr. Linus Morris, *On Expedition*, calls these treasures. Remember the banking illustration we used earlier? God deposits treasures into your account. It is your responsibility to draw upon the treasures God provides.

JOURNAL TIME

Draw a cross in your journal. On the left side of the cross, write about your life before you knew Jesus. On the right side of the cross, write how your life is different now. Tomorrow, we will look at the struggle to stay on the right side of the cross.

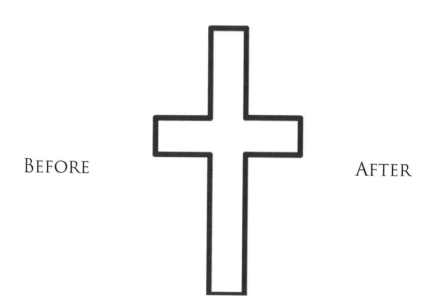

BEFORE   AFTER

WEEK 2—DAY 3
THE STRUGGLE—"NO MORE"
ROMANS 7

THE KEY WORD: "STRUGGLE".

THE KEY POINT: "WE CONTINUE TO STRUGGLE WITH THE FLESH."

Read Romans 7:1-6
PERHAPS YOU ARE FEELING—BUT IT IS NOT WORKING. YOU ARE NOT ALONE.[14]

See footnote # 14. When we teach Kingdom Discipleship, we often use this exercise.

Take a moment and write down what is not working in your life right now.

---

[14] HAVE SOMEONE IN YOUR SMALL GROUP STAND UP AND SAY WAIT A MINUTE, THESE BENEFITS, OR TREASURES, ARE NOT BENEFITING ME. I'M FAILING. PULL UP TWO CHAIRS. HAVE THE PERSON WHO STOOD UP SHARE THEIR STRUGGLE. THEN BEGIN EXPLAINING THE FOUR LAWS (3 IN CHAPTER 7 AND THE FINAL, 4TH LAW, IN CHAPTER 8). THE FOURTH LAW IS THE 10TH TREASURE.

Paul explains in Romans 7 and 8 about four laws.

Read Romans 7:7-25
In Romans 7 Paul introduces the first three laws.
1 God's Law, the written law 7:1
2 The law of the mind, 7:23
3 The law of sin, 7:23

Paul explains how Israel tried and failed to keep God's law, and he extrapolates our failure to keep the written law as well.

The written law serves like a thermometer or a mirror. A thermometer can't heal you, and a mirror can't make you look better. Thermometers and mirrors simply reveal our condition.

The law of the mind refers to the things you know to be true and seek to live out but fail to be able to do. Like the moralist, you can't keep your own laws.

Before I became a follower of Jesus, I was a thief and a liar. I developed a large vocabulary of four letter words. I wanted to stop, I tried to stop, but my self-effort left me disappointed repeatedly. My actions were disconnected from the law of my mind.

The law of sin continues to lie to us and say the life before the cross is better than the life after the cross. Remember sin is a noun, an entity. When we realize our life is rooted in sin resulting in the fruit of sins, we can turn to God. Simply attempting to deal with the fruit, our sins, will not change us. We must be re-rooted, transplanted into a new life in Jesus and filled with his Spirit (We'll pick this up tomorrow).

JOURNAL TIME

How's the battle going for you? Before we talk about the 4th law, take a few moments to reflect about your struggles.[15] Be honest.

---

[15] In your small group this week get into groups of two and share about something you are struggling with, then pray for one another.

WEEK 2—DAY 4
THE EMPOWERING SPIRIT
ROMANS 8

THE KEY WORD: "SPIRIT"
THE KEY POINT: "GOD'S SPIRIT LIVES IN YOU
AND EMPOWERS YOU TO LIVE THE LIFE AS A
DISCIPLE."

Read Romans 8
Verse 1 reveals the 10th Treasure

TREASURE # 10 AND THE FOURTH LAW ARE THE SAME—THE EMPOWERING SPIRIT

The Fourth law: The law of the Spirit of life in Christ Jesus, 8:2

When I was 14 years old, I attended a Full Gospel Business Men's Fellowship International Meeting. Senator Ralph Ellis spoke. After the talk, he invited people to come forward who wanted prayer. I made my way to the front of the room. Privately, I had been asking the Lord about the filling of the Holy Spirit, but when I went forward, I asked Ralph to pray for a family friend who was going through a divorce, and for my brother to quit smoking. Ralph laid hands on me and I do not remember if he prayed for my requests or not. What I do remember, he prayed for me to be filled with the Holy Spirit. I immediately began speaking in tongues and left the meeting somewhat dazed.

What followed over the next few weeks was a set of behavioral changes. I began reading my Bible daily, reading books about growing spiritually, praying for family members and friends, wanting to spend time studying the Bible with others, and I began telling everyone who would listen about Jesus.

Before Ralph prayed over me, I tried really hard to follow Jesus with mixed success. After he laid hands on me, I began to grow and share my faith in a more natural way. My struggles did not disappear, but hunger and thirst for spiritual things definitely increased dramatically.

Romans 8:7, 11, 14-16, 18, 21, 26, 30, 32, 37-39 (ESV)

7 "For the mind that is set on the flesh is hostile to God, for it does not submit to God's law; indeed, it cannot.

11 If the Spirit of him who raised Jesus from the dead dwells in you, he who raised Christ Jesus from the dead will also give life to your mortal bodies through his Spirit who dwells in you.

Romans 8:12-17

14 For all who are led by the Spirit of God are sons of God. 15 For you did not receive the spirit of slavery to fall back into fear, but you have received the Spirit of adoption as sons, by whom we cry, "Abba! Father!" 16 The Spirit himself bears witness with our spirit that we are children of God, 17 and if children, then heirs—heirs of God and fellow heirs with Christ, provided we suffer with him in order that we may also be glorified with him.

Romans 8:18-30

18 For I consider that the sufferings of this present time are not worth comparing with the glory that is to be revealed to us.

21 that the creation itself will be set free from its bondage to corruption and obtain the freedom of the glory of the children of God.

26 Likewise the Spirit helps us in our weakness. For we do not know what to pray for as we ought, but the Spirit himself intercedes for us with groanings too deep for words.

30 And those whom he predestined he also called, and

those whom he called he also justified, and those whom he justified he also glorified.

Romans 8:31-39
32 He who did not spare his own Son but gave him up for us all, how will he not also with him graciously give us all things?

37 No, in all these things we are more than conquerors through him who loved us. 38 For I am sure that neither death nor life, nor angels nor rulers, nor things present nor things to come, nor powers, 39 nor height nor depth, nor anything else in all creation, will be able to separate us from the love of God in Christ Jesus our Lord."

Those who submit to God through a personal relationship with Jesus Christ cannot be separated from God. God adopts us, and we receive his name. Jesus removes our shame and restores our honor. Therefore, since our shame is removed and our honor restored, we can place our mind on these realities. The Fourth Law/10th Treasure is the key to victory.

All of creation longs for restoration with its Creator. When I submitted my will to the filling of the Holy Spirit, bondages began to break. God uses prayer, submission, difficulty, struggles, and relationships to diminish our dependence on our efforts, and increase our yielding to him.

Romans 8:1-2

The law of the Spirit enables us to understand . . .
- We are IN CHRIST Romans 8:3-4
Jesus entered the fray to show us how to walk with God
- The battle is for our minds Romans 8:7-8
If our minds are set on the flesh, life keeps leading to dead ends. Fleshly thinking leads to hostile, combative attitudes and actions not pleasing to God.
- We are part of God's family Romans 8:15
We are daughters or sons of God and his Spirit fills us, we need community, a spiritual family to grow with.

Romans 8:9-15, 26-30, John 14:15-17, 25-26, 15:26-27, 16:7-15

• Suffering refines us and creates in us a longing for our future hope Romans 8:18.

Suffering is never wasted, God uses our suffering to make us more like Christ.

Romans 8:16-25, Titus 2:13

• Nothing external or internal can separate you from the eternal God who loves you Romans 8:37-38

Christ is for us and we cannot be separated from him Romans 8:31-39

10 Treasures of walking by faith

4 Peace
5 Grace
6 Hope
7 Love
8 MUCH MORE—No Wrath
9 MUCH MORE—His Life
10 MUCH MORE—Abundance
11 MUCH MORE—Reign
12 New Life
13 His Spirit

JOURNAL TIME

Write down why you are thankful to God.

Take time to pray and cry out to God to fill you with his Holy Spirit. Take time, don't rush through your prayer time today. Perhaps you need to schedule an extended time for a long walk, or drive. If you are a nature person, go to the beach, mountains, or wherever you feel closest to God. If music speaks to your soul, listen or play some music. Find an environment where you can cry out to God asking him for a fresh filling of his Holy Spirit. I once heard D.L. Moody, a famous evangelist from the 19th Century, said he prayed daily for the filling of the Holy Spirit because he leaks. We, too, leak. Ask God to fill you.

Week 2—Day 5—Review

Read Romans 5-8 again.

Journal Time

What stands out to you as you review this week's lessons?

What did God speak to you?

What action steps are you taking?

Draw the Romans Map and share it with a family member or a friend.

Week 3—Day 1
My Kinsman—Romans 9

The Key Word: "Kinsman".

The Key Point: "Who are those closest to you who need Jesus?"

We now move to the third quadrant—Send. In quadrant #1 God brings us to himself and rescues us, in quadrant #2, he builds us up through the 10 Treasures and restores us. In quadrant #3, a shift occurs, God sends us out to rescue others.

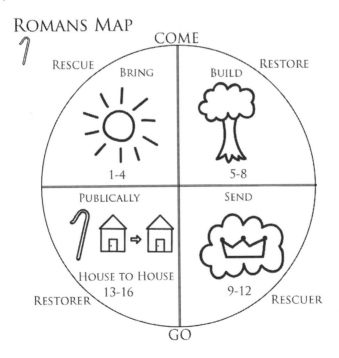

ROMANS MAP

COME

RESCUE

BRING

BUILD

RESTORE

1-4

5-8

PUBLICALLY

SEND

HOUSE TO HOUSE
13-16

9-12

RESTORER

RESCUER

GO

Read Romans 9:1-29
Romans 9:3, 17, 21, 33 (ESV)
3 "For I could wish that I myself were accursed and cut off from Christ for the sake of my brothers, my kinsmen according to the flesh."

Paul is totally committed to seeing his kinsmen know Christ. Who are your kinsmen? Your people?

Joan and I currently live in the town I grew up in, Myrtle Beach, South Carolina. I love surfing. Surfers are my kinsmen. I want to see as many surfers as possible come into a relationship with Jesus Christ.

17 "For the Scripture says to Pharaoh, "For this very purpose I have raised you up, that I might show my power in you, and that my name might be proclaimed in all the earth."

God's heart continues to be for the whole world, "in all the earth." He desires all people to know him, even surfers.

Dennis Cochrane served as a cross-cultural worker in Papua New Guinea. Dennis spoke to a group of college students in my dorm one night about God's heart for the world. I went to him afterwards and asked if he was saying all people should go to the nations. His response deepened my prayer life. He said, "No, I am saying you should pray for the Lord of the harvest to send out laborers into God's harvest field." I started asking God to send laborers into the world. Be careful what you pray for; today, my wife and I work with a cross-cultural team taking the good news of the kingdom to the ends of the earth.

21 "Has the potter no right over the clay, to make out of the same lump one vessel for honorable use and another for dishonorable use? 22 What if God, desiring to show his wrath and to make known his power, has endured with much patience vessels of wrath prepared for destruction, 23 in order to make known the riches of his glory for vessels of mercy, which he has prepared beforehand for glory— 24 even us whom he has called, not from the Jews only but also from the Gentiles?"

God calls people to himself. Who is God calling around you? Look and listen to the people around you and join God in pointing people to him.

A friend of mine prayed one morning to be used by God. He took some scrap metal to the junkyard to be recycled. He noticed an elderly gentleman struggling to empty his pickup truck filled with metal. My friend went over and started helping him. He then looked at the elderly gentleman and said, "Let me do this for you." When my friend finished, the older man looked him in the eye and said, "I prayed God would send someone. You are the answer to my prayers." Who might you be an answered prayer for? God is at work all around you. Ask God to include you in others' stories. Watch to see what happens next.

Romans 9:30-33

33 "as it is written,
'Behold, I am laying in Zion a stone of stumbling, and a rock of offense; and whoever believes in him will not be put to shame.'"
God's heart is to remove our shame. God will never shame those who believe in him.

People all around us carry shame, people in our families, neighbors, strangers at Walmart, friends we eat, play, and work with. Ask God to reveal who needs their shame lifted. When God identifies someone, join God by telling them the good news of the gospel of the Kingdom. The good news of Jesus taking our shame.

If we don't share with others, they will not know the good news. My daughter-in-law, Paula, said when she was teaching this section to a group in California, "No one is going to know Jesus if you never say his name." We must tell others.

We all love our kinsmen, at least most of the time. We desire for those we love to know Christ. Paul emphasizes God's heart for all people and speaks of God's wrath and power. Those who trust in Christ receive power and will not be put to shame, but wrath awaits those who reject God. Notice the turn in section three from the internal benefits, treasures we've received, to the needs of the world around us.

A GLOBAL FOCUS

Romans 9 Shifts from the internal world to the world.

Paul reminds us in Romans 9 of God's Heart for all people. Romans 9:17

Write down a name of someone you love who does not know Christ.

God identifies you as "My People." Romans 9:25-26
Who did God use to bring you to Himself?

Be patient, not everyone responds to God's Invitation the first time. Romans 9:27

Did you respond the first time?

Works, Don't Work. Romans 9:32

In what ways are you still attempting to do good works to be accepted by God?

Do you carry shame? Jesus came to free you from shame. Thank the Lord for taking your shame and placing it upon the cross. Romans 9:33

There are four groups of people in our lives.
- **Family members**
- **Friends**
- **Co-workers**
- **Community**

FAMILY	FRIENDS
CO-WORKERS	COMMUNITY

JOURNAL TIME

Write down three names of people who are far from God in each of the four categories above. They may be indifferent toward God, moralists or religious, but they do not know of the righteousness received by faith.

What is the key to reaching them?

When will you share the good news of the kingdom? Write down a time.

Week 3—Day 2
Sent—Romans 10

The Key Word: "Sent".

The Key Point: "God wants to send you to reach those far from God."

Read Romans 10:1-10
Romans 10:2-3, 11-13, 15, 19 (ESV)
"Brothers, my heart's desire and prayer to God for them is that they may be saved."

Paul commits to pray for the lost.
Follow Paul's example. Don't just have a heart's desire for those you care about to commit their lives to Jesus, pray for them to do so as well.

3 "For, being ignorant of the righteousness of God, and seeking to establish their own, they did not submit to God's righteousness."

Paul realized the religious try to establish their own righteousness.
We become experts at trying to establish our own righteousness. When you hear a person condemning others' behaviors, you have a front row seat to someone seeking to establish their own righteousness.

Romans 10:5-21
11 "For the Scripture says, 'Everyone who believes in him will not be put to shame.' 12 For there is no distinction between Jew and Greek; for the same Lord is Lord of all, bestowing his riches on all who call on him. 13 For 'everyone who calls on the name of the Lord will be saved.'"

Paul made his appeal for belief as the only means to remove shame.

14 "How then will they call on him in whom they have not believed? And how are they to believe in him of whom they have never heard? And how are they to hear without someone preaching? 15 And how are they to preach unless they are sent? As it is written, 'How beautiful are the feet of those who preach the good news!'"

We are messengers of the good news of the kingdom.

19 "But I ask, did Israel not understand? First Moses says, 'I will make you jealous of those who are not a nation; with a foolish nation I will make you angry.'"

Paul wanted to use the community found in Christ as a means of making outsiders jealous.

FAMILY	FRIENDS
CO-WORKERS	COMMUNITY

JOURNAL TIME

Hospitality, developing community, provides a great way for others to know God. Look back at the four windows. Who do you need to invite out for coffee, or lunch? Or invite over for a meal, or a movie?

Who can you include in your faith community?

Write out a hospitality plan.

Several years ago, Joan and I invited a friend, with whom I'd been meeting one-on-one for several weeks, to come to our small group. When he saw the body of Christ loving each other in the setting of shared life in a home, he became a follower of Jesus. Our community evangelism of inclusion proved more effective than my well thought out arguments.

Week 3—Day 3
God's Master Plan
Romans 11

The Key Word: "Plan".

The Key Point: "God's master plan includes Jews and Gentiles."

Read Romans 11:1-10

Romans 11:5, 9, 11, 14, 23, 26, 29, 35-36 (ESV)

5 "So too at the present time there is a remnant, chosen by grace. 6 But if it is by grace, it is no longer on the basis of works; otherwise grace would no longer be grace."

Season your message with grace.

Joan and I stopped by a roadside restaurant on our way back from Virginia. We ordered two ribeye steaks. We waited expectantly at this hole in the wall place thinking we'd discovered a hidden gem; the food looked amazing. However, when we got the steaks fresh off the grill, the taste did not match the anticipation or the appearance. The meat looked good but lacked seasoning. Too often, our presentation of the gospel lacks seasoning.

My son, Nate, pastors in Huntington Beach, California. He and I walked down main street toward the pier one afternoon. He stopped and spoke with multiple homeless people along the way. He knew their names and their stories, and they knew his. Several within the homeless community view Nate as their pastor. He's faithfully seasoned the gospel of the kingdom by engaging and listening to others stories. He's also faithfully shared the good news of Jesus Christ with them. They've seen him perform funerals, weddings, baptisms, and interventions. His heart and his hearth don't serve up seasonless steaks, or sermons.

9-10 "And David says, 'Let their table become a snare and a trap, a stumbling block and a retribution for them; let their eyes be darkened so they cannot see, and bend their backs forever.'"

Paul's hopes in the Jews falling, in their darkness, they will see the need to see light, and be lifted up.

"Let their eyes be darkened" seems a bit sadistic. However, if you recall Paul's journey, you realize he was blinded by the light before he saw the light. Paul hopes the same for those he tries to reach.

Romans 11:11-24

11 "So I ask, did they stumble in order that they might fall? By no means! Rather through their trespass salvation has come to the Gentiles, so as to make Israel jealous."

God's plan includes Jews and Gentiles.

14 "in order somehow to make my fellow Jews jealous, and thus save some of them. 15 For if their rejection means the reconciliation of the world, what will their acceptance mean but life from the dead?"

Together Jews and Gentiles will finally honor God.

23 "And even they, if they do not continue in their unbelief, will be grafted in, for God has the power to graft them in again."

God is orchestrating a master plan of blending Jews and Gentiles for his glory.

Read Romans 11:25-36

26 "And in this way all Israel will be saved, as it is written, 'The Deliverer will come from Zion, he will banish ungodliness from Jacob'; 29 For the gifts and the calling of God are irrevocable."

Israel is still part of God's plan.

35 "'Or who has given a gift to him that he might be repaid?'
36 For from him and through him and to him are all things.

To him be glory forever. Amen."
God will be glorified.

JOURNAL TIME

Write down as many ways as you can think of to reach family members, friends, co-workers, and your community.

Come up with a time-line. Over the next three months how will you implement the plan? Write it out into 12 week periods.

Week 1—I will . . .

Week 2—I will . . .

And so forth . . .

Share your plan with your prayer partner, or small group this week. Pray together for those on your list who do not know God.

Week 3—Day 4
Team—Romans 12

The Key Word: "Team".

The Key Point: "To reach those far from God you need to do so as a team."

Read Romans 12:1-2

Paul speaks of God's grace and favor not being earned. Grace comes as a gift. Remember, gift giving shows honor. God's graces, gifts, his kids as a show of honor. Normally, we view jealousy as negative. But in Romans 12 God's uses jealousy to reach more people. God grafts Gentiles into his kingdom as a gardener grafts tree branches. God even has a no return policy on his gifts; they are "irrevocable".

As a side note, let me address a controversial concept. Paul says "all Israel will be saved." It is important for us to place "all" in the context of the rest of the book of Romans. In Romans 10:13 Paul says "Everyone [all] who call upon the name of the Lord will be saved." The Greek word for "all", πᾶς, is the same in both Romans 10:13 and Romans 11:26. In other words, "all", including Jews and Gentiles, or Muslims, Hindus, Buddhists, Animists, and others, who call upon the Lord Jesus Christ, will be saved. As Jews and Gentiles respond to the gospel, glory goes to God. Paul does not advocate for universal salvation in his use of "all"; rather, in the context of his use throughout the book, "all" refers to all who respond to the invitation of grace.

Here are a few verses I find challenging and compelling.

Read Romans 12:3-8
  Romans 12:3, 6, 9, 14-21 (ESV)
    3 "For by the grace given to me I say to everyone among

you not to think of himself more highly than he ought to think, but to think with sober judgment, each according to the measure of faith that God has assigned."

6 "Having gifts that differ according to the grace given to us, let us use them: if prophecy, in proportion to our faith;"

Our different gifts necessitate our need to function on teams. When we think we don't need other's gifts, we are thinking more highly of ourselves than we should.

Read Romans 12:9-21

9 "Let love be genuine. Abhor what is evil; hold fast to what is good. 10 Love one another with brotherly affection. Outdo one another in showing honor"

13 "Contribute to the needs of the saints and seek to show hospitality."

14 "Bless those who persecute you; bless and do not curse them. 15 Rejoice with those who rejoice, weep with those who weep. 16 Live in harmony with one another. Do not be haughty, but associate with the lowly. Never be wise in your own sight. 17 Repay no one evil for evil, but give thought to do what is honorable in the sight of all. 18 If possible, so far as it depends on you, live peaceably with all. 19 Beloved, never avenge yourselves, but leave it to the wrath of God, for it is written, 'Vengeance is mine, I will repay, says the Lord.' 20 To the contrary, 'if your enemy is hungry, feed him; if he is thirsty, give him something to drink; for by so doing you will heap burning coals on his head.' 21 Do not be overcome by evil, but overcome evil with good."

The heaping of coals on their heads confuses a lot of folks; it seems Paul is being vengeful. However, the opposite is the case, Paul provides a cultural example of how to show honor to your enemies.

In Paul's day, fire gave life; without it, cooking, light at night, and warmth, did not happen. People guarded coals in much the same way, we guard our phone chargers from our teenagers. First century people carried coals in an insulated container on top of their heads. If you've traveled to a majority world country, you likely have seen women carrying objects, with amazing skill, on top of their heads. Heaping of coals on one's head enabled them to carry fire from one base camp to the next. Coals on the head showed kindness not judgment.

Paul provides us with great wisdom, insights, and guidelines to season our message with grace. My dad loved using sayings to teach life principles.

After he died, I wrote down some of his sayings. Here are a few I remember.

- "If you are not 5 minutes early, you are late."
- "If you get a ride with someone, pay for the gas."
- "It's not how much you make; it's how much you save."
- "If you want to change the world, go out into the yard and find a stick. Draw a circle with the stick in the dirt. Get in the circle and change everything in the circle first."
- "If a person wants a job, they are working. If they are not working, they are looking for a position, not a job."
- "Facts you must face whether you like them or not."

Dad's guiding sayings served me well through the years. In a similar way, I picture Paul in Romans 12 giving us 30 guiding principles for effective team function.

1 God gifted you
2 "Don't think more highly of yourself"—We need each other
3 Genuinely love one another
4 Abhor evil
5 Hold fast to the good
6 Love one another and show brotherly affection
7 Outdo one another in showing each other honor
8 Do not be slothful
9 Be fervent
10 Serve the Lord
11 Rejoice in hope
12 Be patient in tribulation
13 Be constant in prayer
14 Contribute to the needs of the saints
15 Show hospitality
16 Bless those who persecute you
17 Bless and do not curse
18 Rejoice with those who rejoice

19Weep with those who weep.
20Live in harmony with one another
21Do not be haughty
22Associate with the lowly
23Never be wise in your own sight
24Repay no one evil for evil
25Honor others in the sight of all
26Live peaceably, as far as it depends on you
27Never avenge yourself
28Leave room for the wrath of God
29Do not be overcome with evil
30Overcome evil with good

JOURNAL TIME

How many people could be reached if you intentionally invested in a few disciples?

How many churches could be planted, if over a lifetime, you faithfully invested in a few—who invested in few—who invested in a few more?

By God's grace and for His glory, what do you sense God would like to do in and through your life in the next 12 months to reach others? Write down at least three things.

Pause and pray for God to speak to you.

Now, for these three things to be accomplished 12 months from now, what three things need to happen six months from now for new followers to be established in their faith? How do you help others grow?

Pause—pray.

For these things to happen 6 months from now, what do you need to do differently in the next 90 days?

Pause—pray.

What do you need to do in the next 30 days?

Pause—pray.

What do you need to do next week?

Write down practical steps you can take.

What do you need to do today?

Name one thing.

In your small group this week chart out the next 12 months together. What could God accomplish through you together in 12 months?

What needs to happen in 6 months?

What do you need to do in the next 90 days?

Next month?

Next week?

Today???

Week 3—Day 5—Review

Read Romans 9-12

Journal Time

How do you move from being rescued and restored to rescuing and restoring others?

Romans 12 mentions seven spiritual gifts. Pick one or two you think you might have and discuss it with your prayer partner. Provide examples of why you picked the one(s) you did.

What action steps have you taken this week?

Week 4—Day 1
Publicly—Romans 13

The Key Word: "Publicly".

The Key Point: "How do we live out our faith in a society far from God?"

We move now to the fourth quadrant. Paul now talks about how we live out our faith in two contexts.
1 Publicly, including secular society, and the larger group of believers.
2 Privately, House to House, both in our families, and when we use our homes as bases for the ministry of hospitality.

Romans Map

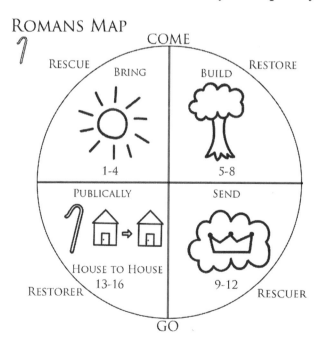

Read Romans 13:1-7

Romans 13:2-4, 7, 9, 13-14 (ESV)

2 "Let every person be subject to the governing authorities. For there is no authority except from God, and those that exist have been instituted by God. 3 For rulers are not a terror to good conduct, but to bad. Would you have no fear of the one who is in authority? Then do what is good, and you will receive his approval, 4 for he is God's servant for your good. But if you do wrong, be afraid, for he does not bear the sword in vain. For he is the servant of God, an avenger who carries out God's wrath on the wrongdoer. 5 Therefore one must be in subjection, not only to avoid God's wrath but also for the sake of conscience."

Paul starts out by saying God uses governments for his glory

Paul is not saying all government is good. He is saying order is better than disorder. Paul writes during a time of political chaos.

Nero, was not exactly a good leader. Nevertheless, Paul knew if the church was to survive, respect for order was needed to effectively spread the gospel of the kingdom. Therefore, he provided much needed guidance.

7 "Pay to all what is owed to them: taxes to whom taxes are owed, revenue to whom revenue is owed, respect to whom respect is owed, honor to whom honor is owed."

Romans 13:8-14

Paul says look, pay your taxes

Joan and I were in dire circumstances years ago unable to pay our taxes. We prayed, waited, and were delighted when a friend showed up unexpectedly with a check covering our expenses. We felt like Peter when Jesus told him to go fishing and he'd find the money he needed to pay his taxes in the fish's mouth. Both Jesus and Paul paid taxes.

9 "For the commandments, 'You shall not commit adultery, You shall not murder, You shall not steal, You shall not covet,' and any other commandment, are summed up in this word: 'You shall love your neighbor as yourself.'"

Love your neighbor

The 10 commandments fall into two categories—Our relationship with God, and our relationship with each other. Jesus tells us to love God and to love one another, thus summarizing the 10 commandments. Paul echoes Jesus' command.

13 "Let us walk properly as in the daytime, not in orgies and drunkenness, not in sexual immorality and sensuality, not in quarreling and jealousy. 14 But put on the Lord Jesus Christ, and make no provision for the flesh, to gratify its desires."

Put on Jesus and quit giving in to the flesh

In week three, we spoke of living life with an open hand toward those in authority over us. Submission to human authority equals submission to God. God wants us to be good citizens. We need to respect those in leadership. Love must remain our central theme. Where love exists, jealousy doesn't. Paul urges us to walk with a clear conscience including how we behave as good citizens.

JOURNAL TIME

When do you find it most difficult to see God working through flawed human institutions and governments?

Can you think of any biblical characters who lived under evil governmental regimes? Was God silent in their circumstances? Did God change their circumstances?

When circumstances didn't change, or got worse, how did God work in and through his people?

WEEK 4—DAY 2
DISPUTABLE MATTERS
ROMANS 14

THE KEY WORD: "DISPUTABLE".
T
HE KEY POINT: "HOW DO WE TREAT THOSE WITH
WHOM WE DISAGREE?"

Read Romans 14:1-12
  Romans 14:6, 11-12, 15-19, 22 (ESV)
   As if dealing with governments wasn't challenging enough, Paul turns to dealing with matters within the church—issues believers disagree on.

   6 "The one who observes the day, observes it in honor of the Lord. The one who eats, eats in honor of the Lord, since he gives thanks to God, while the one who abstains, abstains in honor of the Lord and gives thanks to God."

   What are some issues in your culture over which Christians disagree?

   Paul says we are to seek to show honor to those with whom we disagree. In 2020, the church family Joan and I belong to merged with another church. The new group brought around 150 new people. One of the challenges included the COVID-19 pandemic. One group leaned toward masks, distance, and online platforms. The other group largely ignored masks, social distance, and pushed for face to face gatherings.

How do we show honor to those with whom we disagree?

11 "for it is written, 'As I live, says the Lord, every knee shall bow to me"
12 So then each of us will give an account of himself to God."

We would do well to remember—each of us is accountable to God

Romans 14:13-23
15 For if your brother is grieved by what you eat, you are no longer walking in love. By what you eat, do not destroy the one for whom Christ died. 16 So do not let what you regard as good be spoken of as evil. 17 For the kingdom of God is not a matter of eating and drinking but of righteousness and peace and joy in the Holy Spirit. 18 Whoever thus serves Christ is acceptable to God and approved by men. 19 So then let us pursue what makes for peace and for mutual upbuilding.

- Don't grieve your brother
- Walk in love
- Serve Christ
- Pursue peace
- Build each other up

Joan loves a deal when she goes shopping. The church in Rome was made up of Jews and Gentiles. The Gentiles also loved a deal. They would wait until the food offered to idols went on sale. They would then purchase their chicken at a reduced price. Some believers saw the practice as wise stewardship; Joan would have been in this group. Others saw purchasing sacrificed food as participating in the idol worship.

Paul says, love one another. He encouraged the believers who felt free to buy the reduced produce to not do so when it offended the weaker, more conservative brother or sister who was coming over for dinner.

> 22 "The faith that you have, keep between yourself and God. Blessed is the one who has no reason to pass judgment on himself for what he approves."

Whatever we do we are to honor the Lord
We are to seek that which builds others up
In other words, we honor the Lord by honoring others, not by judging our sisters and brothers.
What About Disputable Matters
Who is the weaker follower?

Look at Romans 14:1 for the answer.
The more conservative?

The less conservative?

What is the grid we should use to measure our freedoms?

Think in terms of a continuum. On the left side of a piece of paper write the word opinion. On the right side, write an item of biblical certainty.

Opinion (Your favorite team for instance)...............Jesus died and rose again.

On the left side of the continuum, we have freedom to disagree, our favorite team. On the right side, we need agreement, the gospel—Jesus' death, burial, and resurrection. We can disagree on the left, but must agree on the right. Fewer issues are on the right than most of us realize.

Most items we argue about fall more toward the left side of the paper. Show honor to those you disagree with. By honoring others, we honor God. Many items in the Bible appear to be cultural. One such example would be head coverings. Foot washing might be another. When we place these items too far to the right, we fall into legalism and dishonor our sisters and brothers we are called to love. These should not be placed on the side of certainty.

Look at Romans 14:6, 12, 15
- Honor
- Remember we will give an account of ourselves to God
- Love

Romans 14:17 (ESV)
Kingdom centered living will produce three things, what are they?[16]

The goal in disputable matters is?
Romans 14:19
Building others up!
When we are building each other up we are not tearing them down or judging them. Jesus warned us about judging others.

"Judge not, that you be not judged." Matthew 7:1

---

[16] Righteousness, peace, and joy.

JOURNAL TIME

What disputable matter challenges you the most right now?

How can you honor God and those you disagree with this week?

What act of kindness can you show to someone with whom you don't agree?

WEEK 4—DAY 3
FOCUS—ROMANS 15

THE KEY WORD: "FOCUS".
THE KEY POINT: "WE NEED TO KEEP OUR
FOCUS ON OUR UNITY TO REACH A LOST
WORLD."

Read Romans 15:1-7

As we saw in the previous chapter we easily get distracted by disputable matters and lose sight of honoring God and others. Paul quickly corrects us and says, get your eyes on Jesus and his heart to reach the world.

Romans 15:1-2, 6-7, 9, 13-15, 19-29 (ESV)

"We who are strong have an obligation to bear with the failings of the weak, and not to please ourselves. 2 Let each of us please his neighbor for his good, to build him up."

Seek ways to build up those you disagree with

6 "that together you may with one voice glorify the God and Father of our Lord Jesus Christ. 7 Therefore welcome one another as Christ has welcomed you, for the glory of God."

Welcome those with whom you differ

Read Romans 15:8-13

9 "and in order that the Gentiles might glorify God for his mercy. As it is written, 'Therefore I will praise you among the Gentiles, and sing to your name.'

Remember God's mercy

13 "May the God of hope fill you with all joy and peace in believing, so that by the power of the Holy Spirit you may abound in hope."

Extend hope

Read Romans 15:14-21

14 "I myself am satisfied about you, my brothers, that you yourselves are full of goodness, filled with all knowledge and able to instruct one another."

Dialogue together

15 "But on some points I have written to you very boldly by way of reminder, because of the grace given me by God"

Extend grace

19 "by the power of signs and wonders, by the power of the Spirit of God—so that from Jerusalem and all the way around to Illyricum I have fulfilled the ministry of the gospel of Christ; 20 and thus I make it my ambition to preach the gospel, not where Christ has already been named, lest I build on someone else's foundation, 21 but as it is written, 'Those who have never been told of him will see, and those who have never heard will understand.'"

Remember our mission is those far from God

Read Romans 15:22-33

24 "I hope to see you in passing as I go to Spain, and to be helped on my journey there by you, once I have enjoyed your company for a while. 25 At present, however, I am going to Jerusalem bringing aid to the saints. 26 For Macedonia and Achaia have been pleased to make some contribution for the poor among the saints at Jerusalem. 27 For they were pleased to do it, and indeed they owe it to them. For if the Gentiles have come to share in their spiritual blessings, they ought also to be of service to them in material blessings.

28 When therefore I have completed this and have delivered to them what has been collected, I will leave for Spain by way of you. 29 I know that when I come to you I will come in the fullness of the blessing of Christ."

Use your resources & energy to extend the gospel not fight with others

When we build each other up, we glorify, honor, God. God empowers us. We are to instruct one another. We are to help the poor. Those who receive spiritual blessings are to bless their teachers with material blessings. We are called to help one another. The concept of blessing fits the honor paradigm well.

JOURNAL TIME

Look over the bullet points listed today. Pick one to focus on and journal about. How can you live it out with those in your faith community?

WEEK 4—DAY 4
MULTIPLY LEADERS
ROMANS 16

THE KEY WORD: "LEADERS".

THE KEY POINT: "TO REACH THE WORLD WE NEED TO RAISE UP MORE LABORERS (LEADERS)."

Read Romans 16:1-16

Romans 16:1-2, 14, 19-20, 25-27
"I commend to you our sister Phoebe, a servant of the church at Cenchreae, 2 that you may welcome her in the Lord in a way worthy of the saints, and help her in whatever she may need from you, for she has been a patron of many and of myself as well."

Paul calls Phoebe a patron in a patron/client world[17]
The church is to help her fulfill her mission

---

[17] Paul closes the book of Romans by speaking of a woman leader named Phoebe. Although he refers to her as a servant, as all leaders are called to be, Paul calls her a patron, not client, in the text. Patrons in a patron/client relationship are the leaders. She helped many, including Paul. One third of the names mentioned in Paul's closing list of leaders are women. God restores honor to both genders in the kingdom. He speaks of obedience resulting in rejoicing. Paul mentions, "Crush Satan under your feet," showing the ultimate reversal introduced in chapter 1. When we honor God, he restores our honor, and Satan is crushed under our feet. The goal of God is to reach all nations by removing their shame and restoring their honor through faith in Jesus Christ. When we partner with God, he is glorified and we experience freedom. All honor to His name.

14 "Greet Asyncritus, Phlegon, Hermes, Patrobas, Hermas, and the brothers who are with them."

They functioned in teams

Read Romans 16:17-24

19 "For your obedience is known to all, so that I rejoice over you, but I want you to be wise as to what is good and innocent as to what is evil. 20 The God of peace will soon crush Satan under your feet. The grace of our Lord Jesus Christ be with you."

The God of peace will crush Satan under your feet
Don't forget we are in a spiritual battle

Read Romans 16:25-27

25 "Now to him who is able to strengthen you according to my gospel and the preaching of Jesus Christ, according to the revelation of the mystery that was kept secret for long ages 26 but has now been disclosed and through the prophetic writings has been made known to all nations, according to the command of the eternal God, to bring about the obedience of faith—27 to the only wise God be glory forevermore through Jesus Christ! Amen."

The goal is all nations; go and proclaim the gospel to all nations!

JOURNAL TIME

Look over the bullet points again today and choose one to focus on and journal about.

Week 4—Day 5
Read Romans 13-16

Journal Time

What did you learn about God in the book of Romans?

What did you learn about yourself?

Who do you need to share with?

What is Your Next Step?

Appendix A

The following five colors and symbols will help you to identify major themes and patterns throughout the Bible.

- Yellow
- Green
- Blue
- Red
- Brown

Your Next Step is a discipleship ministry my wife, Joan, and I started in 2004. Your Next Step grew out of our years of working as church planters. Your Next Step's Mission is:

- **Bring them in**
- **Build them up**
- **Send them out**
- **Publicly, and House to House**

For someone to become a follower of Jesus, a disciple, the Holy Spirit must draw them to the Father through the Son—Jesus Christ. When I became a follower of Jesus Christ, I was nine years old. My burning passion became, "tell others." God uses the process of telling others as his primary way of bringing people into his kingdom.

Bring them in

Bring to the Father (Bring people into the kingdom)

Yellow Sun

The symbol of "the sun" and the color "yellow" represent bringing others into the light.

"For the Son of Man came to seek and to save the lost." **Luke 19:10 (ESV)**

Jesus said to him, "I am the way, and the truth, and the life. No one comes to the Father except through me. **John 14:6 (ESV)**

Take your colored pencils, find Luke 19:10 and John 14:6 in your Bible. Once you locate the two verses highlight both verses using your yellow pencil. These two verses epitomize God bringing others into the light of his love. After underlining or highlighting the verses in yellow, draw the symbol of the sun under or beside each verse as a reminder to yourself of God's desire **to bring others into his kingdom.**

When you share your story of coming into a relationship with Jesus Christ with others, God will use your experience to bring other people into the light of his love. The Bible frequently uses the metaphor of "walking with God" to describe our relationship with him. God uniquely designed you and your story so others can join you in walking in the light. Who do you know who is currently walking in darkness? Who needs to hear your story?

BUILD THEM UP

Build others up in the Son (Build them up, or grow them up in the Kingdom)

Green Tree

For we are God's fellow workers. You are God's field, God's building. **1 Corinthians 3:9 (ESV)**

I grew up in a resort city, Myrtle Beach, South Carolina. During my childhood, I remember new homes and new hotels constantly popping up like mushrooms—new buildings everywhere; my father owned a couple of those properties. However, dad came to city life late in life. When he was 51, he left farming for resort life. Paul, who wrote the book of Corinthians—quoted above—lived during a time when many people made their living through what they grew, but Paul also lived during a time when cities like Corinth were expanding rapidly. Paul mixes his metaphors in the verse above by using a rural agricultural example and a city example—God's field, God's building to describe the process of disciple making. We too use both ideas here, build them up—and then we show the tree as our image for growth—"God's field, God's building".

Kingdom Discipleship borrows from Paul's language and uses the concepts of building and growing interchangeably. God desires for you to grow, to spread out, to build, to multiply.

And what you have heard from me in the presence of many witnesses entrust to faithful men who will be able to teach others also. **2 Timothy 2:2 (ESV)**

Look up the 1 Corinthians 3:9 and 2 Timothy 2:2 in your Bible. Highlight the two verses in green. Then draw the symbol of the tree under or beside each verse in your Bible.

SEND THEM OUT

Send in the power of the Holy Spirit to proclaim the kingdom

 **Blue Sky with a crown.** The crown represents the kingdom. The cloud signifies our stepping outside into the world to declare the kingdom (Presumably under a blue sky).

And I heard the voice of the Lord saying, "Whom shall I send, and who will go for us?" Then I said, "Here I am! Send me." **Isaiah 6:8 (ESV)**

And Jesus came and said to them, "All authority in heaven and on earth has been given to me. Go therefore and make disciples of all nations, baptizing them in the name of the Father and of the Son and of the Holy Spirit, teaching them to observe all that I have commanded you. And behold, I am with you always, to the end of the age." **Matthew 28:18-20 (ESV)**

Look up Isaiah 6:8 and Matthew 28:18-20 in your Bible and highlight these two passages in blue. Then draw the symbol of the crown and the cloud under or beside each passage.

God gifts each of us to accomplish his mission in and through us. He sends us out as gifted people to serve him and others. As we go out, may he give us blue skies. In America, we use a phrase, "The sky's the limit," meaning we seek to reach out as far as possible. God desires for us to reach out beyond our people group to multiply disciples, leaders and churches around the world.

PUBLICLY

Publicly

Red Shepherd's Staff

How I did not shrink from declaring to you anything that was profitable and teaching you in public and from house to house. **Acts 20:20 (ESV)**

I am the good shepherd. The good shepherd lays down his life for the sheep. **John 10:11 (ESV)**

In 2008 I traveled to India for the first time. I met a man who quoted a couple of mission statements from large churches in the United States. How he memorized mission statements from churches thousands of miles away in a completely different culture baffled me. He asked me to tell him my mission statement. I said, "Bring them in, Build them up, Send them out, Publicly and House to House." He indicated he liked my statement. Then I asked him for his mission statement. I was unprepared for his answer. He said, "Greater love has no one than this, Jesus died for me, and I will die for him." In 2017, he and his wife both died. Jesus said a good shepherd lays down his life for the sheep; they willing give their blood to spare the sheep. In honor of my friend who was a good shepherd, I use red, indicating a disciples willingness to spill their own blood for Jesus, as the color for the shepherd's staff.

Leadership takes place in both private and public settings. The Scripture uses the metaphor of a shepherd to refer to leaders. Moses, David, Jesus, Peter, and Paul each speak of leaders shepherding people. God calls us to be shepherds. He invites us to follow him by laying down our selfish dreams, agendas, desires, and very lives if necessary.

Look up Acts 20:20 and John 10:11 in your bible and highlight the verses in red, then draw a shepherd's staff beside or below the verses in your bible.

HOUSE TO HOUSE

House to House

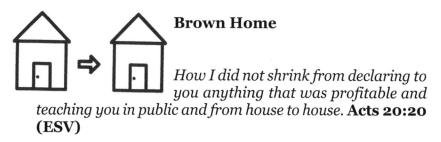

Brown Home

How I did not shrink from declaring to you anything that was profitable and teaching you in public and from house to house. **Acts 20:20 (ESV)**

In traveling throughout North, Central, and South America, Europe, Africa, and Asia, I've seen homes of varying shapes and sizes. However, in each location, I noticed earthen homes and wooden structures with a natural brown color—therefore, we use brown to highlight "house to house." Journal a picture of your house.

Leadership starts at home. The home is where we begin making disciples. Joan and I married on 19 October 1986; we began using our home as a base for ministry from the beginning. **The home is a place where we cannot hide who we really are.** What would happen if your home became a center for ministry? Take a moment to journal any thoughts you have about using your home to minister to others.

"And they sang a new song, saying, 'Worthy are you to take the scroll and to open its seals, for you were slain, and by your blood you ransomed people for God from every tribe and language and people and nation, and you have made them a kingdom and priests to our God, and they shall reign on the earth.'" **Revelation 5:9-10 (ESV)**

The mission is to *Bring them in, Build them up, Send them out Publicly, and House to House.* The following chart gives examples of how to highlight your Bible according to these themes.

     Bring them in	EVANGELISM God is Loving and is in Charge	**God as Father** Love, Grace, Reconciliation, Sin, Salvation, Sovereignty, Creator, Sacrifice, Atonement, Redemption, Baptism, Justification, Missions
     Build them up	DISCIPLESHIP He has a Kingdom	**God as Son,** Revelation, The Word, Sanctification, Suffering, Growth, Money, Kingdom, Spiritual Warfare (Kingdoms in conflict), Personal Prayer, Health, Time Management, Sexuality, The Second Coming, Judgment
     Send them out	MINISTRY His Kingdom Expands through His People (Both Israel and the Church)	**God the Holy Spirit,** Gifting, Talents, Abilities, Israel as a People, the Church, Service, Helping the Poor, Caring for Our Planet
     Publicly	WORSHIP (PRIVATE AND PUBLIC) God's People Need Leaders	**Leaders** Public prayer, Worship, giving, leaders, leadership, Roles of Men and Women, Hearing God's Voice
     House to House	FELLOWSHIP Leadership starts in the home	**Families** Homes as Places for Ministry, Meals, Family, Husband and Wife, Children

Let's practice highlighting using the color code.

Turn in your Bible to Acts 2:42-47. Read through the passage and with your colored pencils highlight the themes you observe. Two examples are provided for you.

Example 1—Verse 43 has blue because signs and wonders, miracles occur in this verse. When the apostles went out (Hint— under blue sky . . . memory technique—they proclaimed the kingdom). The apostles were sent out to proclaim and demonstrate the kingdom—they were sent out.

Example 2—Verse 47 points to people being brought into a right relationship with the Father—they were brought in.

Acts 2:42-47 New American Standard Bible (NASB)

⁴² They were continually devoting themselves to the apostles' teaching and to fellowship, to the breaking of bread and to prayer.

⁴³ Everyone kept feeling a sense of awe; and many wonders and signs were taking place through the apostles.

⁴⁴ And all those who had believed were together and had all things in common;

⁴⁵ and they *began* selling their property and possessions and were sharing them with all, as anyone might have need.

⁴⁶ Day by day continuing with one mind in the temple, and breaking bread from house to house, they were taking their meals together with gladness and sincerity of heart,

⁴⁷ praising God and having favor with all the people. And the Lord was adding to their number day by day those who were being saved.

JOURNAL TIME

Use your journal to write down:
Bring them in—Who brought you to Jesus Christ?

Build them up—How are you growing in your relationship with God?

Send them out—Who do you need to share Jesus with?

Publicly and House to House—Who needs you to shepherd them?
When can you invite them over to your home?

ABOUT THE AUTHOR

We live between the inauguration of the kingdom, "the already", and the consummation of the kingdom, "not yet." Kingdom Discipleship seeks to make more and better disciples until Jesus return. Douglas and Joan Dorman formed Your Next Step as a discipleship ministry in 2004 after 17 years as church planters. Turning Disciples into Disciple Makers describes the lives of Douglas and Joan Dorman. Together, they teach, train, mentor, and coach others in discipleship, prayer, and leader development. The Dormans utilize a relational—life on life—approach to discipleship and emphasize the importance of using one's home as base for ministry. They have seven children and a growing number of grandchildren.

Douglas completed his Ph.D. in Intercultural Studies at Biola University and Joan graduated with a BSN is nursing from the University of North Carolina Chapel Hill. Douglas and Joan currently serve as Senior Staff with Global Training Network. For more information, visit: www.gtn.org.

To schedule discipleship training with your group email Doug at: dougd@gtn.org

Made in the USA
Columbia, SC
02 November 2022

70355006R00061